CONTENTS

KT-461-273

INTRODUCTION

In the game of golf, a ball is played from the tee into the hole by successive strokes according to a set of rules. One round of the course is the usual length of a match, but in some competitions two or more rounds are played. One round takes about three hours to complete.

THE PROFESSIONAL GOLFERS' ASSOCIATION (PGA)

The PGA is a members' organisation with over 7,500 qualified professionals, who employ around 1,000 registered assistants. The Association is dedicated to training and serving golf professionals, who offer a highly efficient service to amateur golfers at clubs, driving ranges and other golf establishments.

To become a PGA member, assistants must spend a period of three years working with a PGA professional at a club or driving range. During this time, they must attend courses of instruction, complete distance learning assignments and pass examinations. Once they are qualified, graduates can apply for full membership. The PGA offers various opportunities for members to gain further qualifications.

For further information, please write to: The Professional Golfers' Association, Centenary House, The Belfry, Sutton Coldfield, West Midlands, B76 9PT, or visit: www.pga.info.

FULL-SIZED COURSES

A full-sized course consists of 18 holes, usually split as follows:

- four short holes, which measure up to 250 yds (230m) from tee to green, and can be covered by one full stroke

- fourteen longer holes, approximately 250–500 yds (230–450m) in length, and requiring two or three full strokes from tee to green.

The space between tee and green at the long holes is occupied by mown turf called the fairway. On either side of the fairway are rough grass, trees and bushes. There are also hazards of various kinds, mainly sand bunkers but occasionally streams, ditches and ponds. The green is a closely mown surface for putting, and the hole is sunk in the green and marked with a flag.

Produced for A & C Black by

Monkey Puzzle Media Ltd
Gissings Farm, Fressingfield
Suffolk IP21 5SH

Published in 2007 by

A & C Black Publishers Ltd
38 Soho Square, London W1D 3HB
www.acblack.com

Fifth edition 2007

Note: While every effort has been made to ensure that the content of this book is as technically accurate and as sound as possible, neither the author nor the publisher can accept responsibility for any injury or loss sustained as a result of the use of this material.

This book is produced using paper that is made from wood grown in managed, sustainable forests. It is natural, renewable and recyclable. The logging and manufacturing processes conform to the environmental regulations of the country of origin.

Acknowledgements
Cover and inside design by James Winrow and Tom Morris for Monkey Puzzle Media Ltd.
Cover photograph of Tiger Woods teeing off on the ninth hole during the third round of the Western Open, 2006 courtesy of AP/PA Photos (Jeff Roberson). Photos on pages 9, 18, 20, 21, 22, 23, 25, 26, 27, 28, 29, 31, 33 and 35 courtesy of Alex Hazle/Axel Design & Photo. Photos on pages 54 and 55 courtesy of Getty Images. All other photos courtesy of Empics. Illustrations by Dave Saunders.

The publishers would like to thank Laraine Beeching for her contribution to this book and Gareth Williams, PGA Professional at Donnington Grove Country Club, for his expert advice and modelling in Alex Hazle's photographs.

KNOW THE GAME is a registered trademark.

Printed and bound in China by C&C Offset Printing Co., Ltd.

Note: Throughout the book players and officials are referred to as 'he'. This should, of course, be taken to mean 'he or she' where appropriate. Similarly, all instructions are geared towards right-handed players – left-handers should simply reverse these instructions.

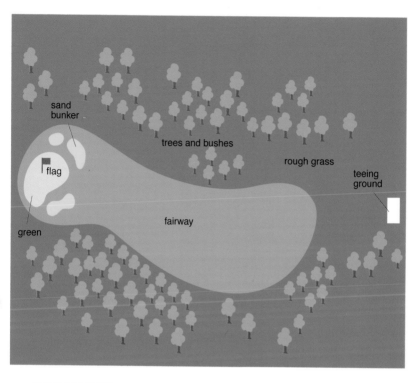

sand
bunker

trees and bushes

rough grass

flag

teeing
ground

fairway

green

Layout of a typical hole
on a golf course.

RULES OF THE GAME

This book is an
introductory guide to the
game of golf and is not
meant to be a complete
reference. Rules are
summarised on pages
38–48. The official Rules
of Golf are governed by
the Royal and Ancient
Golf Club (R&A) of St
Andrews. A complete set
of rules is available at
www.randa.org.

**The hole
is 4 in (108mm)
in diameter and
at least 4 in
(100mm)
deep.**

ETIQUETTE

Golf has a code of etiquette, which should be observed by all golfers and studied carefully by beginners. Observing these rules of behaviour makes the game more enjoyable. The rules of etiquette are summarised as follows but for a more detailed explanation, see pages 50–51.

THE 'TEN COMMANDMENTS'

These are golf's most important rules, and all players need to be aware of them before going out on the course.

1. Always play without undue delay. If your match has lost one complete hole, ask the match behind to play through, and stand well to the side as they do so. The same applies if your match loses a ball.

2. Do not play a stroke until the match in front is out of range. Use a warning cry of 'Fore!' if the ball goes anywhere near a fellow player.

3. Always stand well clear of the person making a stroke, for your own safety and to avoid distracting the player by obscuring his or her vision. Stand still and remain quiet, facing the player if you can.

Before playing a stroke or making a practice swing, ensure that no one is standing close by or in a position to be hit by the club or the ball.

Even the pros have to yell 'Fore!' now and again. Here, Phil Mickelson gives the warning.

Always replace your divots – especially if they are huge, like this one from Tiger Woods.

4. Divots should always be replaced. Holes and footmarks in bunkers must be smoothed out with the rake provided.

5. Bags must not be laid on the green, because they may cause damage.

6. Trollies should be left well to the side of the green to avoid damage to the surrounds.

7. The first player to hole out on the putting green should retrieve the flag and be ready to replace it in the cup when the last player has holed out.

8. Scorecards should be marked up on the next tee and not on the putting green.

9. In the absence of special rules, two-ball matches have precedence over three- and four-ball matches. A single player playing should give way to a match of any kind.

10. Do not move, talk, stand too close to or directly behind a player when a stroke is being played.

> **When balls are in play, the ball furthest from the hole is played first.**

EQUIPMENT – CLUBS

Golf clubs must conform to clearly defined specifications and design principles, as determined by the governing bodies. Clubs are not permitted to be adjustable, except for weight.

TECHNICAL DESCRIPTIONS

Clubs need to conform to the rules so no unfair advantage is gained. An example is driver regulations where the clubface must not act like a spring when the ball is hit. For golfers governed by the R&A nonconforming clubs will be outlawed from 2008.

There are various regulations for woods and irons, including:

- length – a minimum of 18 in (45.7cm) and not longer than 48 in (122cm)
- head dimensions and size – woods must not exceed 28.06 cubic in (460cm³)
- the markings and roughness on the face
- the straightness of the shaft and where it is attached to the clubhead
- the grip – which must be circular, except for a small rib and it cannot be moulded to the hands.

Putters have different regulations. They can be longer, the shaft does not have to be attached to the heel of the head and the grip may have a flat section.

THE 3 BASIC TYPES OF CLUB

- Wood – a broader headed club, previously made of wood, now more often made of metallic materials.
- Iron – a narrower-shaped, steel-headed club.
- Putter – a club designed primarily for use on the putting green.

The distinctive head shape of a driver, as shown by Annika Sorenstam.

CLUB SPECIFICATIONS

Each club is designed to do a different job. The length of a club varies from approximately 43 in (109cm) for a driver to 35 in (89cm) for a short iron. As the club length reduces, the face angle (or 'loft') increases, which helps to hit higher but shorter shots.

- A driver will have around 9 to 13 degrees of loft.

- A 5 iron will be around 38 in (97cm) and have 27 degrees of loft.

- A wedge will be around 35 in (89cm) and have 48 degrees of loft.

Women's clubs are usually lighter and slightly shorter than men's clubs. The shafts tend to have more bend or flex, the grips are generally thinner too. The same also applies to junior clubs.

CLUB SELECTION

Numbers on the head of an iron indicate what kind of use it is intended for. A 3 iron will usually be the longest iron and have the least amount of loft, producing a longer, lower shot. A higher number will be shorter in length and have more angle to hit higher but shorter distances.

A selection of irons. The different shapes and lengths are designed for different types of shot.

CHOOSING YOUR CLUBS

The maximum number of clubs permitted is 14, but a full set is not necessary to start with. A beginner can start with a single iron – a 6 or 7 is best. Some clubs can be bought individually and they will often be provided when taking lessons.

To begin playing on the course a set consisting of some irons – numbers 4, 6, 8 and PW (pitching wedge) are a good combination – a putter, a wood and a small bag is perfectly adequate. Some excellent-value starter packages are available, in full and half sets, although to begin with you may well not use all the clubs in a full set.

If buying second-hand clubs, ensure that a PGA professional checks they are suitable. There are a number of points to be considered when purchasing clubs.

Clubhead design
Some irons have a thin base (sole) and a flat back; these are known as blades, and tend to be preferred by good players, who favour their look and the feel they provide. If a blade is not hit correctly, a great deal of distance and direction will be lost. Other irons have weight moved to the outside of the head so a cavity is formed; they tend to have a wider sole and are slightly offset in the neck. These features mean that less distance and direction is lost on poorly hit shots.

Drivers in particular have bigger heads; they are often made of a metal called titanium, which is both light and strong, meaning they can be made larger. The head is also hollow, so weight can be distributed to make them more forgiving.

JUNIOR CLUBS

Juniors should use junior clubs as they will have lightweight shafts, heads and thin grips – they are designed to help the swing develop. A cut-down adult's club will only hinder progress.

PGA professionals are trained to 'custom fit' clubs to players' requirements.

Paula Cramer chooses the driver from her bag. Her nickmane is 'Pink Panther' (the head cover is a giveaway!).

Shaft type

Shafts tend to be made of either steel or graphite. They also have varying amounts of flex (bend) and torque (twist). The correct shaft is one that is suited to a player's swing style and the speed the club is swung at. Getting advice from a club professional will be useful in deciding this.

Club length

Tall people do not necessarily need longer clubs and vice versa for short people. A longer club may help to gain extra distance, but if it is too long the player may lose control and be unable to hit shots in the centre of the face.

CLUB FLEX

A club's 'flex' is shown on the shaft:
L = most flexible
A or 'senior' = medium flex
R = regular flex
S = stiff flex
X = extra stiff flex

Be sure to check your clubs regularly, particularly the grips and where the head joins the shaft.

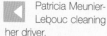
Patricia Meunier-Lebouc cleaning her driver.

Lie angle

This is the angle at which the shaft extends from the head when the centre part of the sole is resting flat on the ground. The angle at which the club returns to the ball for impact can affect the direction the ball flies – the correct lie angle is therefore crucial. If the toe end is pointing up at impact, the ball is likely to travel left of target; this lie angle would be too upright and a flatter lie would be required. If the heel is pointing up at impact, the lie is too flat and the club needs to be made more upright. A PGA professional can check the lie and make any adjustments.

Grip type and thickness

Grips are made from rubber compounds. Some have cord in them, which provides a good grip but is harsh on the hands. Oversize and soft-feel grips are available; these might suit a player with joint problems such as arthritis. Grip size is important for player comfort and controlling the wrist action in the swing.

Set make-up

Some players may benefit from extra woods, wedges or hybrids; these are a blend of woods and irons.

EQUIPMENT – THE BALL

Like clubs, golf balls must conform to clearly defined specifications. The weight of a golf ball cannot be greater than 1.62 oz (45.9g), and it must be at least 1.68 in (42.7mm) in diameter.

TYPES OF BALL

There are four types of ball – one-, two-, three- and four-piece.

One-piece balls
One-piece balls, as the name suggests, are moulded in one solid piece; they are usually used on driving ranges and not really suitable for the course.

Two-piece balls
Two-piece balls have a core and outer dimpled cover. Dimples help the ball to fly through the air better. These are a good choice for a player seeking extra distance, but less backspin will be produced, so they are harder to stop on the green. Two-piece balls are very durable and are less expensive to purchase.

Three- and four-piece balls
Three-piece balls have a core, an inner cover and dimpled cover. They are a good combination ball, providing distance, spin and feel; however they tend to be more expensive to buy. A four-piece ball usually has two parts to the core, the inner cover and finally the outer cover.

EQUIPMENT CHECKLIST

- clubs (maximum 14)
- bag (and trolley/cart if necessary)
- balls
- tees
- glove (optional, though recommended)
- ball markers
- pitch repairer
- head covers (to keep clubheads clean and dry)
- towel (especially to keep club shafts dry)
- waterproof clothing
- umbrella
- golf shoes (preferably spiked)
- sun visor (optional, though useful)

Teeing off the
first hole.

**Don't always
just tee up between
the markers; you can
use the teeing ground's
2-club depth to find a
nice flat grassy
area.**

THE TEEING GROUND

This is the starting place
from which a hole is played.
It is a rectangular area two
club-lengths in depth, the
front and sides of which are
defined by the outside
limits of markers.

The teeing ground is not
necessarily the whole of
the flat space prepared for
teeing, but only that part
in use for the day. The
position of the markers
is varied from day to day
to avoid wear and tear.

GOLF CLOTHING

Golf clothing has changed a great deal since the sport began. You rarely see a pair of plus fours on the course today. Instead, specialist fabrics and designs can now been seen almost everywhere.

THE BASICS

It is worth checking with a club before you play there to see whether they have any particular dress codes. However, the following outfit is likely to be accepted at most courses:

- shirt – the most popular varieties are short-sleeved polo shirts or long-sleeved roll necks

- trousers – you can wear normal trousers, but many sports brands make golf-specific trousers in fabrics designed to dry quickly if it rains. These are cut in a style that best suits a golfer's movements

- shorts and skirts – these are acceptable during the warmer months, but clubs will often stipulate that they must be tailored.

And a jumper is always worth packing too!

SHOE CLEANING

Most courses will have shoe-cleaning facilities at the club house. It may seem a hassle, buts it's always worth cleaning your shoes after a round – they will last longer, and you will get a little more respect next time you take to the first tee.

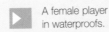
A female player in waterproofs.

SHOES

A good pair of golf shoes will probably be your most important piece of attire. Not only will they be mandatory at many clubs, but they are also a wise investment when you consider that a round of golf could easily see you walk 5 miles (8km).

There are golf shoes to suit all budgets and fashion tastes. Whichever you go for, here are some points to consider:

- studs – golf shoes have studs on the soles. Shoes with rubber – rather than metal – studs are more comfortable and create less damage to the greens

- fit – have your shoes properly fitted: it's difficult to focus on your game when you have painful blisters!

- wet feet – consider a pair of waterproof shoes, to keep your feet dry.

WATERPROOFS

It's worth considering packing a set of waterproofs – or at least a good umbrella – in your golf bag if there is even a possibility that it might rain. They are lightweight and don't take up much room. You'll be happy to have them if you get caught in the rain in the middle of the course.

GLOVES

Most golfers wear a glove to improve their grip on the club.

- Buy a glove for the hand that is uppermost on the grip, i.e. right for a left-handed player and left for a right-handed player.
- Gloves come in a variety of sizes and materials – it's best to ask the shop pro for advice when buying one.

 Ernie Els (left) and Ian Poulter display the two extremes of golfing fashion.

COACHING TIPS

Although each golf shot has its own nuances, there are some general points that can be applied to all or most scenarios. These will be helpful in developing a strong technique, as well as in analysing where your shots can be improved.

CAUSE AND EFFECT

This is a summary of basic coaching points and the reasons behind them. With these, as with the shot techniques given on the following pages, it can be useful to rehearse them with the help of a qualified coach.

Aim
The blade needs to be square at right angles to the ball-to-target line, because this encourages a straight flight of the ball.

 Grip, seen from the front and the side.

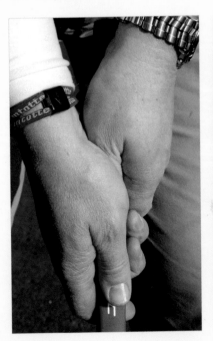

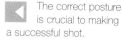
The correct posture is crucial to making a successful shot.

Hold

The hold on the club is taken in such a way as to encourage a square clubface and maximum power at impact. There are more details on pages 20 and 21.

1. If an overlapping grip is preferred, then the small finger of the right hand should be resting in the gap between the middle and forefinger of the left.

2. For the interlocking grip the forefinger of the left hand and the little finger of the right can be lightly intertwined.

Stance

The width of stance, together with the correct posture (see below) will help you to establish good balance.

Posture

Taking the correct posture also gives you the mobility and adaptability needed to play each individual shot.

Body alignment

A parallel stance is needed so that the motion of your arms and the club, together with your body rotation, can create the correct path needed to hit the ball straight towards the target.

Ball position

The ball is placed between your feet to help establish the correct swing direction and angle of attack through impact. (The correct ball position plays a major role in good body alignment.)

PUTTING

Putting is the first skill many golfers learn. Once you can put well, it is possible to build on your technique to add increasing amounts of distance to your shots, until you are able to drive the ball down the fairway.

GOOD PUTTING

The idea is to roll the ball along the ground into the hole using a smooth, unhurried motion that gives control of both distance and direction.

TECHNIQUE FOR A STRAIGHT PUTT

Club selection: Putter

1. Introduce a ball to the target line (the direct line to the hole).

You can aim the putter using an 'H' card pinned to the turf.

2. Point the putter-head towards the hole. When it is at right angles to the target line, the putter-head is said to be 'square to the target line'. The 'H' card, which is shown in the photo (left), can be used in the first instance.

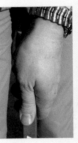

3. (For a right-handed player:) Hold the palm of your left hand opposite the left side of the grip, then close your fingers and hand round the grip with the thumb down the centre of the shaft (see photos above).

4. With your right palm facing the right side of the grip, do the same with your right hand. The right hand should fit closely below the left. Grip pressure should be light and even.

5. Standing erect with feet together, and the arms out in front of the chest with the club shaft parallel to the ground, bend forward from the hip. Your back should remain fairly straight, but not tight.

6. As the clubhead reaches the floor, allow the knees to flex slightly. Take a small step with each foot to the side, to create balance and comfort. Your feet will be a little narrower than shoulder width. Your chin should be slightly raised from your chest.

BODY ALIGNMENT

- Your shoulders, hips, knees and feet should ideally be parallel to the ball-to-target line. The ball should be positioned in the centre of the stance (i.e. with your feet equidistant).
- This encourages the correct shape of swing.

PRACTISING PUTTING

Once you have the correct body position and alignment, you are ready to practise putting. This begins with the swing.

7. The lower half of your body acts as a steady base. All the movement comes from the shoulders rocking the arms and putter back and forth. The length of the swing should be roughly the same both back and through.

8. The distance the ball travels is governed by the length of swing and a consistent rhythm back and forth.

9. The direction the ball travels is mainly controlled by the position of the clubface at impact, as well as the direction the clubhead is travelling in.

Correct body alignment. The clubs on the ground show the 'square stance' position you should adopt.

Address viewed down the target line.

 Address viewed from face on.

Backswing.

Follow-through.

PUTTING PRACTICE

- Start next to the hole, 1 ft (30cm) away and work backwards, every 2 ft (60cm) up to 20 ft (6m), to gain a feel for distance.
- Place four balls around the hole – north, south, east and west – and putt them in from 1 ft (30cm) through to 3 ft (90cm).
- Putt from various distances to the edge of the green. Try to have the ball nestle on the fringe.

To develop the correct 'feel' for putting, get into position without the club. Put your hands together in a 'prayer' position, fingertips pointing at the ground. Move the triangle of arms this creates back and forth like a pendulum.

CHIPPING

The chip shot is generally played from just off the green. It enables the ball to fly over any uneven ground and land on the putting surface, where it can roll to the hole.

CHIPPING CLUBS

The club you use at first is usually a 7 iron. Later on, you might choose a pitching wedge instead, to add a little variety to the shape of the shot:

- 7 iron: ball rolls more than it flies (25 per cent flight, 75 per cent roll)

- pitching wedge: ball flies more than it rolls (75 per cent flight, 25 per cent roll).

Choosing clubs for a chip shot: 7 iron or pitching wedge? It depends how far you want the ball to loft.

When playing a chip shot, holding lower down the grip gives more control.

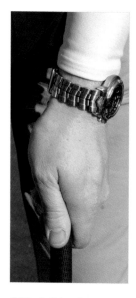

Left-hand grip position.

Left hand viewed from down the target line.

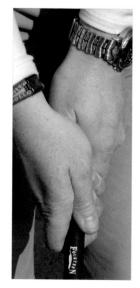

Grip for chip/full swing.

TECHNIQUE FOR A CHIP SHOT

Club selection: 7 iron or pitching wedge

The main change in technique from a putt is that you must create a more descending blow at impact, which allows the ball to fly into the air. As in putting, the clubhead should be square to the target. (The leading edge of the club should be at right angles to the target).

1. Hold the club as for a putt. However, due to the more rounded grip, the left thumb should be slightly more to the right of centre, and the right thumb rests to the left of centre.

2. At this stage you can choose between a ten-finger grip, or an overlapping or interlocking grip.

CHIPPING

The best advice for players working on their chipping is to keep it low, but not too slow: 'low' – a low stance with knees bent, and the ball nearer your back foot; 'slow' – hit through the ball, but with a lower cadence to your swing.

3. Your stance and posture should be as for the putting set up, but place more weight (70 per cent) on your left leg (for a right-handed player). Your hands will be close to your left thigh.

4. Place the ball in the middle of the stance. This, combined with the weight on the left leg, will encourage a more descending blow.

5. Use the same pendulum style swing as for putting. Your weight should remain on the left leg.

6. At the finish, more weight will be on the left leg than at address and the right knee will have moved closer to the left. The right foot may well have rolled onto the instep.

7. The descending blow and the loft on the club combine to get the ball into the air.

Distance and direction in chip shots are controlled in the same way as for putting.

▲ Address for the chip shot viewed from both angles; body alignment is as for putting. The yellow lines show the 'square stance' position you should adopt.

PRACTICE FOR THE CHIP SHOT

- Kneel down, then toss a ball underarm on to the green and observe the roll. This should help you to visualise how the ball reacts on the green.
- Pick a spot on the green, approximately 1 yd (90cm) from the edge, and try to land the ball there. Watch how the ball rolls. (You could use a small towel to identify the landing spot.)

Chip shot: the sequence shows the address, backswing and the finish.

PITCHING

The pitch shot is needed as you move even further back from the green. In general this is a shot that will fly further than it rolls. For this shot, your wrists start to hinge more because of added motion, and the clubhead will be above your hands for the first time.

TECHNIQUE FOR A PITCH SHOT

Club selection: pitching wedge (or a sand wedge can be chosen to give additional height to the flight of the ball).

1. Hold the club as described in chipping (pages 24–27). By varying the height at which your hands are holding on to the grip, you will help change the distance the shot travels:

• lower down – shorter distance

• higher up – closer to maximum distance.

2. Posture is as for putting and chip shots. However, the stance is wider than for a chip shot: adjust your feet so that they are only inside shoulder-width apart.

3. Your body should be aligned to the ball as for chip shots: square to the ball.

◀ A wider stance is needed for a pitch shot.

 Alignment for pitching. The yellow lines show the 'square stance' position you should adopt.

Ball position, in the middle of the stance.

4. As with a chip shot, more weight goes on to the left leg (for a right-handed player), but the distribution is more balanced, at about 60-40 left-to-right.

5. The ball is played in the middle of the stance. This, together with the weight favouring the left leg, will help ensure a descending blow.

PITCHING

Devote plenty of time to practising pitch shots, because they can turn an average round into a good one. It is also important to note how the ball is lying, because this will determine which particular type of pitch shot you can play.

6. As your body turns and your arms swing back, the extra motion will encourage your wrists to hinge in the backswing.

7. At halfway back, the left arm will be level to the floor and your wrists should have hinged the club so that it is approximately 90° to your left arm (for a right-handed player). Your weight will have shifted back, to be more over your right foot.

8. In the downswing, as your arms and the club return through a similar position to that of the address position, your weight should flow back on to the left leg.

9. The follow-through should mirror the backswing in both length and shape.

10. Distance control and direction will be achieved in the same way as in putting and chipping.

Many players think that chipping and pitching are the same thing. In fact, they are different shots. When pitched, the ball spends more time in the air than it does on the ground, whereas a chip will travel further along the ground than it does in the air. A pitch shot is best used when there is an obstacle in the way.

PRACTISING THE PITCH SHOT

- Following on from the chip, do the same underarm toss exercise. This will show you how the motion needs to increase in size to cover more distance.
- Make two practice swings brushing the club on the grass where the ball will be (picture an aeroplane coming into land, touching down and then taking off again – without a crash landing! – as a way of imagining the right amount of contact).

If you are struggling to strike the ball correctly or are unable to turn through to the target, it may help to withdraw the left foot (for a right-handed player) slightly.

Face-on view
of a pitch shot.

Down-the-line view
of a pitch shot.

THE FULL SWING

The full swing is the golf technique that gives you the most distance to your shots. It is a development of the putt, chip shot and pitch shot.

FULL SWING TECHNIQUE

Club selection: 7 iron
(slight adjustments may be required when introducing other clubs at a later stage).

To create a swing that allows you to achieve the maximum distance with each club, while maintaining a high percentage of accuracy, the following technique can be employed. In many ways it is simply a further development of the basic pitching stroke.

1. Your aim should be square to the ball-to-target line.

2. Hold the club at the top of the grip, in the same manner as for pitching.

3. The stance should be approximately shoulder-width wide and the weight distributed 50-50.

4. The posture is just as for all the other shots.

5. Your body alignment should be such that your feet, knees, hips and shoulders are all aligned parallel to the ball-to-target line.

6. The ball position varies depending on the club you are using, from between the centre of the feet to up towards the left foot. It is best to get advice from a coach about where best to place each club, but here are some examples:

- pitching wedge – just left of centre

- 5 iron – left of centre

- 1 wood – just inside left heel.

THE LONGEST BALL

Some golfers are able to drive a golf ball amazing distances. The most incredible of all was the record-setting drive by Mike Austin in September 1974. Austin, who was 64 years old, drove the ball an amazing 515 yds (471m).

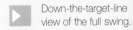
Down-the-target-line view of the full swing.

As the swing progresses from the basic pitch length, there are a few main points you will probably need to remember.

1. In the backswing, your upper body will rotate further round. It can twist through as much as 90°. The hips can twist through approximately 45°. The arms and club will end up over the right shoulder.

2. During the downswing and follow-through, it is important to maintain the sensations from the pitch shot, of which the full swing is a development.

3. The finish position is achieved when:

   a) your upper body and hips are turned towards the target area, with your balance more or less entirely on your left foot (if you are a right-handed player)

   b) your right foot is up on tiptoe and your knees together

   c) at the same time, your arms will be over and above your left shoulder, and the club will be moving behind your back.

It is important to finish the full swing in balance: otherwise, your technique lacks control.

KEEP IT STRAIGHT

There's a saying in golf: 'you drive for show'. Many golfers get caught up with the idea that they have to drive the ball as far as possible off the tee. However, a quick look at the PGA statistics shows that the players with the highest driving accuracy top the overall rankings far more often than the longest drivers. Lesson: think accuracy first, distance second.

Face-on view of full swing.

KEEPING SCORE

Scorecards are used for marking a competitor's score in a medal (strokeplay), Stableford or matchplay-against-par (bogey) competition.

TYPES OF SCORING

- Medal play (strokeplay) – a competitor's full handicap is deducted from the total score.

- Matchplay competition – the winner is decided by the number of holes won.

- Stableford competition – players earn points based on how many shots it has taken them to finish a hole.

In matches, the player with the higher handicap usually receives ¾ of the difference between his handicap and that of his opponent.

SCORECARD BREAKDOWN

Each hole is numbered (and sometimes named), and two distance measurements are usually given to indicate the length of each hole:

1. the distance from the tournament (white) tees

2. the distance from the non-tournament (yellow) tees.

The par for each hole is listed, and the stroke index for each hole is indicated in red. This is an indication of where handicap strokes are taken in matchplay against par (bogey) or Stableford competitions.

The player's score is measured in strokes. This is always given as the gross score – the number of strokes actually played – and inserted by the marker. Handicap calculations are made afterwards.

The final column of each hole shows the results of each hole compared with par.

- If the player's net score for the hole (after deducting any handicap stroke) is less than the par score, the mark is '+', indicating a win.

- If the score is the same, the mark is '0', indicating a halved hole.

- If the score is higher than par, the mark is '-', indicating a loss.

Both the player and marker must sign the card before it is handed in.

COMPETITION		DATE	TIME	Handicap	Strokes Received
Player A			Please indicate which tee used		
Player B			PAR 72 S.S.S. 71 / PAR 72 S.S.S. 69		

Hole	Marker's Score	Name	White Yards	Yellow Yards	Par	Stroke Index	Score A	Score B	W=+ L=- H=0 points
1		Elizabeth 1	330	318	4	13			
2		Paine	191	151	3	7			
3		Templehill	491	471	5	9			
4		Lodgehill	465	422	4	3			
5		Joseph Woods	471	443	4	1			
6		Byron	174	160	3	15			
7		Crackendell	312	302	4	5			
8		Cats Gallows	383	363	4	11			
9		Prince Regent	148	132	3	17			
OUT			2965	2762	34				

Hole	Marker's Score	Name	White Yards	Yellow Yards	Par	Stroke Index	Score A	Score B	W=+ L=- H=0 points
10		Icehouse	550	510	5	12			
11		Walker	493	476	5	16			
12		Cipriani	353	324	4	4			
13		Enzo	342	328	4	18			
14		Caroline Lamb	221	194	3	8			
15		Four Gates	384	363	4	6			
16		Waterfall	422	402	4	2			
17		Avenue	330	305	4	14			
18		Broadwater	509	484	5	10			
IN			3604	3386	38				
OUT			2965	2762	34				
TOTAL			6569	6148	72				

HANDICAP

NETT

Marker's Signature...

Player's Signature...

Holes Won..............

Holes Lost..............

Result.....................

STABLEFORD POINTS OR PAR RESULT

An example scorecard. Note the stroke index: in matchplay or Stableford competitions, a player having a 12-stroke handicap takes one stroke at the 10th hole (stroke index 12) and one each at all other holes having a stroke index less than 12 (i.e. the 2nd, 3rd, 4th, 5th, 7th, 8th, 12th, 14th, 15th, 16th and 18th). A player having only a three-stroke handicap takes them at the 4th, 5th and 16th holes.

A scorecard.

Most of us have to keep our own score – then again, most of us would not want our score displayed quite so prominently!

37

RULES OF THE GAME

Studying the complete rules of golf at the same time as you are improving your technique will help you to become a better all-round player. This section summarises and further explains some of the rules of golf that have been mentioned previously.

GENERAL PENALTY

The penalty for the breach of a rule is the loss of a hole in matchplay or two strokes in strokeplay.

PRACTICE DURING PLAY

During the play of a hole, a player must not play any practice stroke. Between the play of two holes a player cannot play a practice stroke from any hazard, but may practise putting or chipping on or near the green of the hole last played, a practice green or the teeing ground of the next hole to be played.

Players must not agree among themselves to waive a rule, local rule or any penalty incurred.

Assistance or protection includes bending back an obstructing bush or shielding a player from wind or rain.

ADVICE AND ASSISTANCE DURING PLAY

A player may only give advice to, or ask advice from, his or her partner or either of their caddies. A player may have the line of play indicated by anyone (except on the putting green, where only the player's partner or their caddies may do so).

INFORMATION ON STROKES TAKEN

A player who has incurred a penalty must tell his or her opponent as soon as possible. The number of strokes a player has taken includes any penalty strokes.

DISPUTES

In matchplay where there is a dispute about the rules or the number of strokes taken, a claim must be made before the players strike off from the next teeing ground.

In strokeplay no penalty may be imposed after the results are posted, unless a player knowingly returns a score for a hole lower than actually achieved.

ORDER OF PLAY ON THE TEE

A match begins by each side playing a ball from the first teeing ground in order of the draw or by lot. The side which wins a hole plays first at the next teeing ground.

Hitting the ball out of bounds can be very frustrating, even if the scenery is amazing! See page 44 for more information.

If any point in dispute is not covered by the rules or local rules, the decision is made in accordance with fair play and logic.

PLAYING OUTSIDE THE TEEING GROUND

In matchplay there is no penalty for playing the ball from outside the teeing ground. (The stroke may be recalled by the opponent, however.) In strokeplay the player is penalised two strokes and must replay the stroke from the correct place.

ORDER OF PLAY

In matchplay, if a player tees off when his or her partner should have done, the stroke may be recalled by the opponent. In strokeplay there is no penalty for playing out of turn, unless it is to give one player an advantage.

If a player strikes the ball more than once he or she counts the stroke and adds a penalty stroke – making two strokes in all.

Carefully moving a leaf without touching the ball.

LOOSE IMPEDIMENTS

Loose impediments are natural objects, which may be removed without penalty except when both the impediment and the ball lie in or touch the same hazard. When a ball is moving, a loose impediment on the line of play cannot be removed.

> **The ball should be played as it lies at all times except where the rules or local rules provide otherwise.**

PLAYING A WRONG BALL OR PLAYING FROM A WRONG PLACE

A player must hole out with the ball played from the teeing ground unless he or she was permitted to substitute a ball. The penalty for playing a wrong ball is two strokes in strokeplay or loss of the hole in matchplay. There is no penalty for playing a wrong ball from a hazard.

> **A player may stand outside the teeing ground to play a ball within it.**

IMPROVING LIE OR STANCE AND INFLUENCING THE BALL

Irregularities in the surface of the course that could affect a player's lie may not be removed or pressed down, except:

- when fairly taking stance
- in making the stroke
- when teeing a ball
- in the repair of old hole plugs or ball marks on a green.

If a ball lies in long grass, only so much can be touched as will enable the player to find and identify the ball – nothing may be done to improve its lie.

A player may not improve the line of play, the position or lie of the ball or the area of intended swing by bending, moving or breaking a fixed or growing object (except in taking a fair stance to address the ball, and in making the stroke).

LIFTING, DROPPING, PLACING, IDENTIFYING OR CLEANING THE BALL

Through the green or in a hazard, when a ball is lifted under a rule or local rule, or when another ball is to be played, it should be lifted and dropped as near as possible to the spot where the ball lay, except when a rule permits it to be dropped elsewhere or placed.

- In a hazard a lifted ball must be dropped and come to rest in the hazard. If it rolls out of the hazard it must be re-dropped without penalty.

- A ball may only be dropped by the player, who must stand erect, hold the ball at shoulder height and drop with an out-stretched arm. If a ball is dropped in any other way and the mistake is not corrected, the player incurs a penalty stroke.

- A ball to be lifted under the rules may be lifted by the player or his partner, or by another person authorised by the player. It may be lifted for the purpose of identification but must then be replaced on the same spot.

- A ball may be cleaned when lifted from an unplayable lie, for relief from an obstruction, from casual water or ground under repair, from a water hazard, on a wrong green, or on the green.

BALL INTERFERING WITH PLAY

A player may have any other ball lifted if he or she considers that it might interfere with his or her play or assist the play of another player.

A MOVING BALL

A player must not play while the ball is moving, except when it is moving in water, provided the ball is hit without undue delay.

BALL IN MOTION STOPPED OR DEFLECTED

If a moving ball is accidentally stopped or deflected by any outside agency, it is a 'rub of the green' and the ball is played as it lies, without penalty.

If a player's moving ball is stopped or deflected by the player, his or her partner or their caddies, clubs or other equipment, the player is penalised two strokes in strokeplay and loses the hole in matchplay. Aside from a stroke played from a green, if two balls in motion collide, each player plays his or her ball as it lies.

Rule 20-2c gives the seven occasions when a player is required to re-drop a ball.

BALL UNFIT FOR PLAY

If a ball is so badly
damaged that it becomes
unfit for further play, it may
be changed by the player
after agreeing with the
opponent or marker. Mud
on a ball does not make it
unfit for play.

A ball being placed on the
green after being cleaned.

 Lee Westwood and Colin Montgomerie looking for a lost ball.

BALL AT REST MOVED

If a player, his or her partner, or either of their caddies moves the ball, the player incurs a one-stroke penalty. The ball must then be replaced, otherwise the player incurs a second penalty stroke, making two altogether. If it is not possible to determine where the moved ball originally lay, the spot must be estimated and the ball dropped, not nearer the hole.

If a ball is moved by a player's opponent (or their caddies), the player incurs no penalty. If this occurs during a ball search, the opponent incurs no penalty either.

If the opponent moves the ball other than during a search, however, the opponent incurs a one-stroke penalty.

BALL LOST, OUT OF BOUNDS OR UNPLAYABLE

If a player decides the ball is unplayable he or she can either play from where the previous stroke was made, drop a ball within two club lengths of the point where the ball lay (but not nearer the hole), or drop a ball behind the point where the ball lay, keeping the flag in line. All these are under a one-stroke penalty.

PROVISIONAL BALL

If a ball might be lost outside a water hazard or may be out of bounds, a player can at once play another ball provisionally from as near as possible to the spot at which the original ball was played. The player must announce that he or she intends to play a 'provisional ball'.

Tiger Woods drops a ball after finding it unplayable.

OBSTRUCTIONS

- Any movable obstruction may be removed before a shot is played.
- If the obstruction is immovable, and interferes with the lie of the ball, the player's stance, or area of intended swing, the ball may be lifted and dropped not more than one club-length away from the nearest point of relief from the obstruction.
- The ball is dropped, without penalty, and must come to rest not nearer the hole.
- If the ball lies in or on a movable obstruction, it may be removed and the ball dropped in the place directly underneath where the ball lay.

The player is the sole judge as to whether a ball is unplayable.

CASUAL WATER

If a player's ball lies in casual water, he or she may drop a ball, without penalty, on ground which avoids these conditions.

If a ball lies on the green and in casual water, or if casual water intervenes between the ball and the hole, it may be lifted and placed, without penalty, on the nearest spot (not nearer the hole) with a clear line to the hole. This place may be off the green.

HAZARDS AND WATER HAZARDS

When the ball lies in or touches a hazard or water hazard, before making a stroke, the player cannot touch the ground or water in the hazard with the club, nor touch or move any loose impediments in the hazard.

If the ball lies in or is lost in a water hazard, the player can play the ball as it lies or, under a one-stroke penalty, drop a ball:

- behind the hazard, keeping the point where it just crossed the margin of the hazard in line with the flag – there is no limit to how far behind the hazard the player can drop the ball

- where the previous stroke was played from.

Additionally, if the ball last crossed the margin of a lateral water hazard the player may drop a ball within two club lengths of the point where the original ball last crossed the margin of the hazard, or two club lengths from a point on the opposite margin of the hazard equidistant from the hole.

THE FLAGSTICK

Before or during a stroke, a player may have the flagstick removed or held up to indicate the position of the hole. This may be done only on the authority of the player before he or she plays the stroke.

A penalty occurs if a player's ball strikes the flagstick when it is attended or has been removed, strikes the person standing at the flagstick, or strikes an unattended flagstick when played from the green. The player loses the hole in matchplay, or two strokes in strokeplay.

If the ball is played from off the green and comes to rest against the flagstick when it is in the hole, the player is entitled to have the flagstick removed. If the ball falls into the hole, the player is deemed to have holed out.

 Michelle Wie takes a drop from casual water in a bunker.

 Nick Dougherty gets his feet wet to save a stroke.

THE PUTTING GREEN

There are definite rules about care of and behaviour on the putting green, which after all is where many matches are resolved. Crucially, the line of the putt must not be touched, except as provided in the rules.

- A player may place the club in front of the ball when addressing it, without pressing anything down.

- The player may move any loose impediment on the putting green by picking it up or brushing it aside, without pressing anything down.

- The player may repair damage on the putting green caused by the impact of a ball and old hole plugs.

- A ball nearer the hole on the putting green that might interfere with play should be marked and lifted by the opponent or fellow competitor.

- During play of a hole a player must not roughen or scrape the surface or roll a ball to test the surface of the putting green.

The caddie attends the flag.

Great care must be taken by all players to protect the green, in order to keep it in pristine condition.

BEHAVIOUR ON THE COURSE

Golf has very clear rules about behaviour on the course. It is important for all players to understand these rules, which are intended to make the game enjoyable for everyone – not least because infractions can be severely dealt with!

COURTESY ON THE COURSE

All players are expected to behave in a courteous and considerate way to one another, whether part of the same party or not.

- The player who has the 'honour' should be allowed to play before his or her opponent or fellow competitor tees the ball.

- No one should move, talk or stand close to or directly behind the ball or the hole when a player is addressing the ball or making a stroke.

- Players should play without delay.

- No player should play until the players in front are out of range.

- Players searching for a ball should signal the players behind them to pass as soon as it is apparent that the ball will not easily be found. They should not continue play until the players following them have passed and are out of range.

- When the play of a hole has been completed, players should immediately leave the putting green.

PRIORITY ON THE COURSE

On crowded courses it is not unusual for one group of golfers to catch up to another. Who takes priority when this happens?

- In the absence of special rules, two-ball matches should have precedence over and be entitled to pass any three- or four-ball match.

- A single player has no standing and should give way to a match of any kind.

- Any match playing a whole round is entitled to pass a match playing a shorter round.

- If a match fails to keep its place on the course and loses more than one clear hole on the players in front, it should invite the match following to pass.

CARE OF THE COURSE

Players are expected to look after the course as far as possible as they make their round.

- Before leaving a bunker, a player should carefully fill up and smooth over all holes and footprints.

- Through the green, a player should ensure that any cut or displaced turf is replaced and pressed down.

- Damage to the putting green made by a ball should be carefully repaired. Damage to the putting green caused by golf shoe spikes should be repaired on completion of the hole.

- Players should ensure that, when putting down bags or the flagstick, no damage is done to the putting green and that neither they nor their caddies damage the hole by standing close to it, in handling the flagstick or in removing the ball from the hole.

- The flagstick should be properly replaced in the hole before the players leave the putting green.

- Players should not damage the putting green by leaning on their putters, particularly when removing the ball from the hole.

- Local notices regulating the movement of golf carts should be strictly observed.

- In taking practice swings, players should avoid causing damage to the course, particularly the teeing ground, by removing divots.

Tiger Woods rips a huge divot as he chops a shot from the rough.

COMPETITIONS – THE MAJORS

The 'Majors' are the four most prestigious annual tournaments in golf. It is the ultimate ambition for any professional golfer to do the 'grand slam' and win all four tournaments in one year. In the history of golf, this feat is very much a rarity: in the modern game Tiger Woods is the only player to have come close to achieving it.

THE MEN'S MAJORS

The tournaments that have made up the Majors have changed over the years. The original four were: The Open Championship, The British Amateur Championship, the US Open and the US Amateur. Bobby Jones was the only player to complete the grand slam of these titles, doing so in 1930.

It is not known exactly when the current tournaments became the Majors, but they are now: the Masters (held in April at the Augusta National Golf Club, USA); the US Open (held in June); the Open (held in July); and the PGA Championship (held in August in the USA).

Some of these tournaments date back over a hundred years, so it would take a book in itself to list all the winners. These are the Major winners of modern times.

The Masters
1990 Nick Faldo (Eng)
1991 Ian Woosnam (Wal)
1992 Fred Couples (US)
1993 Bernhard Langer (Ger)
1994 José Maria Olazábal (Esp)
1995 Ben Crenshaw (US)
1996 Nick Faldo (Eng)
1997 Tiger Woods (US)
1998 Mark O'Meara (US)
1999 José Maria Olazábal (Esp)
2000 Vijay Singh (Fiji)
2001 Tiger Woods (US)
2002 Tiger Woods (US)
2003 Mike Weir (Can)
2004 Phil Mickelson (US)
2005 Tiger Woods (US)
2006 Phil Mickelson (US)

US Open
1990 Hale Irwin (US)
1991 Payne Stewart (US)
1992 Tom Kite (US)
1993 Lee Janzen (US)
1994 Ernie Els (RSA)
1995 Corey Pavin (US)
1996 Steve Jones (US)
1997 Ernie Els (RSA)
1998 Lee Janzen (US)
1999 Payne Stewart (US)
2000 Tiger Woods (US)
2001 Retief Goosen (US)
2002 Tiger Woods (US)
2003 Jim Furyk (US)
2004 Retief Goosen (US)
2005 Michael Campbell (NZ)
2006 Geoff Ogilvy (Aus)

The Open
1990 Nick Faldo (Eng)
1991 Ian Baker-Finch (Aus)
1992 Nick Faldo (Eng)
1993 Greg Norman (Aus)
1994 Nick Price (Zim)
1995 John Daly (US)
1996 Tom Lehman (US)
1997 Justin Leonard (US)
1998 Mark O'Meara (US)
1999 Paul Lawrie (Sco)
2000 Tiger Woods (US)
2001 David Duval (US)
2002 Ernie Els (US)
2003 Ben Curtis (US)
2004 Todd Hamilton (US)
2005 Tiger Woods (US)
2006 Tiger Woods (US)

PGA Championship
1990 Wayne Grady (Aus)
1991 John Daly (US)
1992 Nick Price (Zim)
1993 Paul Azinger (US)
1994 Nick Price (Zim)
1995 Steve Elkington (Aus)
1996 Mark Brooks (US)
1997 Davis Love III (US)
1998 Vijay Singh (Fiji)
1999 Tiger Woods (US)
2000 Tiger Woods (US)
2001 David Toms (US)
2002 Rich Beems (US)
2003 Shaun Micheel (US)
2004 Vijay Singh (Fiji)
2005 Phil Mickelson (US)
2006 Tiger Woods (US)

THE WOMEN'S MAJORS

The Women's Tour also has four 'Majors'. They are: Kraft Nabisco Championship; LPGA Championship; the US Women's Open; and the Women's British Open.

Kraft Nabisco Championship
2001 Annika Sorenstam (Swe)
2002 Annika Sorenstam (Swe)
2003 Patricia Meunier-Lebouc (Fra)
2004 Grace Park (S Korea)
2005 Annika Sorenstam (Swe)
2006 Karrie Webb (Aus)

LPGA Championship
2001 Karrie Webb (Aus)
2002 Se Ri Pak (S Korea)
2003 Annika Sorenstam (Swe)
2004 Annika Sorenstam (Swe)
2005 Annika Sorenstam (Swe)
2006 Se Ri Pak (S Korea)

US Women's Open
2001 Karrie Webb (Aus)
2002 Juli Inkster (US)
2003 Hilary Lunke (US)
2004 Meg Mallon (US)
2005 Birdie Kim (S Korea)
2006 Annika Sorenstam (Swe)

Women's British Open
2001 Se Ri Pak (S Korea)
2002 Karrie Webb (Aus)
2003 Annika Sorenstam (Swe)
2004 Karen Stupples (Eng)
2005 Jeong Jang (S Korea)
2006 Sherri Steinhauer (US)

JUNIOR GOLF

Gripping it and ripping it, as former Open champion John Daly describes golf, has never been easier for juniors. There are now many different ways to start your golfing career at a young age.

GOLF FOUNDATIONS

There are 268 Golf Foundation starter centres based at the UK's clubs. These are ideal for anyone starting to play; more information is available on their website at: www.golf-foundation.org.

OTHER WAYS INTO GOLF

Many clubs and schools operate the Golf Foundation's Tri Golf, which is a fun and easy introduction to golf. Local golf clubs sometimes run special summer-holiday clinics aimed at young people. Newcomers to golf will also find attitudes changing within golf clubs, with many operating more child-friendly policies than in the past. This is reflected in discounted rates, special tees and access to the course with little or no restrictions.

The Grass Roots Golf Tour is a nationwide golf tour for kids of all ages and abilities to compete and learn how to play the game. More information is available on the website at: www.grassrootsgolftour.com.

PGA PROS

Swindon's Broome Manor professional Barry Sandry is a good example of the work done by PGA pros across the country. Barry won the Golf Foundation's 2006 Sinclair Award for his outstanding contribution to junior golf, which each year sees him coach hundreds of youngsters from aged four upwards.

Former champion golfer Nick Faldo giving a group of lucky children some golf tips.

Broome Manor's reputation as a mini-golfing nirvana for kids is reflected in the fact they have access to an 18-hole course, two nine-hole courses, a par three course, a Tiny Tigers course and two pitch-and-putt courses. Among the most popular is the nine-hole Tiny Tigers course, which stands 950 yds (850m) long and is set on one of the existing nine-hole layouts.

With its own card and rules, juniors as young as four play regular medals, getting used to playing on fairways and greens. As part of the rules, the children have a maximum of 10 shots and four putts on the green.

JUNIOR GOLF IN SCOTLAND

One of the most ambitious junior initiatives is Scotland's clubgolf scheme which has targeted introducing every nine-year-old north of the border (some 50,000) to golf by 2009.

JUNIOR GOLF IN WALES

Wales hosts the Ryder Cup in 2010, and money is being ploughed into grassroots golf initiatives, including helping thousands of children discover golf.

JUNIOR GOLF IN ENGLAND

At national level in England, golf's leading bodies have created the England Golf Partnership. Its aims include building on existing introductory programmes and making England the leading golf nation in the world by 2020.

> **Juniors interested in taking up golf should contact their local PGA professional to find out more about opportunities in their area.**

 A young golfer in the middle of a lesson with a PGA pro.

GOLF CHRONOLOGY

Golf is one of the oldest sports, and has traditions that go back hundreds of years. It has come a long way since the first ball was hit – here are some (but by no means all) of the important milestones that have occurred along the way.

1457 The first written reference to golf can be found in a Scottish Parliamentary order banning the sport, as it was interfering with archery practice (seen to be more important because Scotland was still at war with England!). The ban was lifted in 1502.

1553 The Archbishop of St Andrews issues a decree allowing locals to play golf on the links of St Andrews.

1720s This decade saw the manufacture of a new type of golf ball, the 'featherie'. It was made of leather and stuffed with feathers (prior to this, golf balls had been wooden).

1744 The first golf club was established: the Honourable Company of Edinburgh Golfers. They played one tournament a year in Leith. The club also established the first code of rules to govern play.

1759 The first reference to strokeplay can be found at St Andrews. Prior to this, all play was matchplay.

1764 St Andrews is reduced from a 22-hole to an 18-hole course, the first such and the template for all future courses.

1766 The first club outside Scotland was established by a group of expatriate Scots in Blackheath, Kent. This was followed 20 years later by the first club in the United States, in South Carolina.

1810 The earliest recorded reference to a women's competition in Musselburgh, Scotland.

1850s This decade saw a new ball being developed: the 'gutty'. It was cheaper to manufacture than the 'featherie' and a lot harder, which led to the development of iron-faced clubs. It was also cheaper to buy and travelled further when hit.

1857 The first book on golf instruction is published. It is *The Golfer's Manual* by H.B. Farnie.

1860 The first Open Championship took place in Prestwick, Ayrshire. It was won by Will Park of Musselburgh, who played the three rounds of the 12-hole course in 174 shots. The competition was opened to amateurs as well as professionals the following year.

1867 The first club for women is founded: the Ladies' Golf Club at St Andrews.

1880 Moulds are used to give the 'gutty' balls dimples, thus improving their aerodynamics.

1890 John Ball becomes the first amateur and non-Scot to win the Open Championship.

1895 The US Open is played for the first time and is won by Willie Anderson. It is the same year that the USGA (formed the year before) bans the use of the pool cue as a putter!

1898 Coburn Haskell patents the 'Haskell ball', the first to have a rubber core.

1901 The Professional Golfers' Association (PGA) (Great Britain & Ireland) is established.

1902 The first groove-faced irons are invented.

1905 William Taylor patents the first dimple pattern for golf balls.

1910 Arthur F. Knight patents steel shafts for clubs.

1912 John Ball wins his eighth British Amateur Championship, a record that still stands.

1914 Harry Vardon wins his sixth Open Championship, which is still a record.

1916 The PGA of America is formed and the PGA Championship is inaugurated. The first winner is James Barnes.

1927 The first official Ryder Cup takes place between the US and Britain, with the US winning 9 to 2.

1933 The Augusta National Golf Club opens for play. Also in this year, Craig Wood hits a whopping 430-yd (393-m) drive at the British Open, which remains the longest drive in a Major.

1934 The first Masters is played and is won by Horton Smith. The USPGA Tour also begins in this year.

1950 The Women's Professional Golf Association is replaced by the LPGA.

1960 Lifting and cleaning the ball on the putting surface is allowed for the first time.

1963 Arnold Palmer becomes the first professional player to earn over $100,000 in official prize money in a calendar year. Five years later he became the first player to pass $1,000,000 in career earnings.

1964 The World Matchplay Championship is played for the first time at Wentworth.

1971 Astronaut Alan Shepard hits a 6 iron on the Moon.

1972 Spalding introduce the first two-piece ball, the Top-Flite.

1973 The graphite shaft is invented.

1976 Judy Rankin become the first female professional to earn $100,000 in a season.

1979 The Ryder Cup is altered to allow European players to join the British team. The first metal woods are also introduced in this year.

1986 Jack Nicklaus wins his 18th Major, the Masters – a record that still stands.

1987 Europe wins the Ryder Cup on American soil for the first time.

1988 Curtis Strange becomes the first professional to earn $1,000,000 in prize money in a season.

1997 Tiger Woods wins his first Major, the Masters, at a record age of 21 years and three months.

2001 Tiger Woods completes the 'Tiger Slam', holding all four Majors at the same time (although not in the same year to constitute the ultimate grand slam).

2004 Michelle Wie becomes the youngest woman to play at a PGA event, at just 14 years of age.

Michelle Wie watches her drive on the second tee during the first round of the Kraft Nabisco Championship golf tournament, 2006.

GLOSSARY

Address A player has 'addressed the ball' when he has taken his stance and grounded his club.

Birdie A score of one under par for a hole.

Bogey A score of one over par for a hole.

Caddie A person who carries a player's clubs and assists him or her in accordance with the rules.

Casual water Any temporary accumulation of water that is visible before or after the player takes his or her stance and which is not in a water hazard.

Committee The group in charge of a competition.

Competitor A player in a stroke competition.

Divot The grass removed when playing an iron shot.

Fairway The short, mown grass between the tee and the green. Either side of the fairway is the rough, where the grass is longer.

Flagstick A movable pole centred in the hole to show its position.

Green The finely manicured area surrounding the hole. This area is designed for putting.

Handicap A system of scoring that allows good players and less-able players to compete on equal terms. Your first handicap will probably be 36. This means that when you finish playing, you deduct 36 strokes from your score. As you get better, your handicap is reduced.

Hazard A bunker or water hazard.

Honour The side which is entitled to play first from the teeing ground is said to have the 'honour'.

Hook For a right-handed golfer, a shot that starts to the right of the target and curves dramatically to the left, usually ending much further left of the target than was desired.

Lie The resting position of the ball after it has been hit. The middle of the fairway is a good lie. A ball in the rough or half-buried in a bunker is a bad lie.

Loose impediment A natural object that is not fixed or growing, such as stones, leaves, twigs and branches.

Marker A scorer in strokeplay who is appointed by the committee to record a competitor's score.

Matchplay In matchplay, a hole is won by the side which holes its ball in the fewest strokes (after deducting any handicap allowance). The hole is halved if each side holes out in the same number of strokes. A match consists of a stipulated round or rounds, and is won by the side which is leading by a number of holes greater than the number remaining to be played.

Observer A person who assists the referee and reports any breach of the rules.

Par The number of shots a good player is expected to take either on a given hole or for an 18-hole round.

Partner A player associated with another player on the same side.

Penalty stroke A stroke added to the score of a side under certain rules.

Provisional ball A ball played as a potential replacement for a ball that may be lost or out of bounds.

Rub of the green A rub of the green occurs when a ball in motion is stopped or deflected by an outside agency.

Slice For a right-handed golfer, a shot that starts to the left of the target and curves to the right.

Stipulated round This consists of playing the holes of the course in their correct sequence unless otherwise authorised by the committee. The number of holes in a stipulated round is 18, unless a smaller number is authorised by the committee.

Strokeplay In strokeplay, the competitor who completes the stipulated round or rounds in the fewest strokes is the winner. In stroke competitions under handicap, the full handicap allowed to the player is deducted from his or her total, and the net score counts.

Tee The small wooden or plastic pin on which the ball sits when the first shot is played on each hole.

Teeing ground The starting place for the hole to be played.

Water hazard Any sea, lake, pond, river, ditch, surface drainage ditch or other open-water course (whether or not containing water).

INDEX